Ro & the Places She Goes

by

La Shuana Rochelle Cole

Dedication

This book is dedicated to everyone with a disability. Whether it is visible or invisible, remember these words: disabilities are not debilitating.

Acknowledgment

Thanks to my mom for her constant support and encouragement, not only throughout the creation of this book, but throughout my life. Also, thank you to the friends and others who supported, encouraged, advised, and offered help to me throughout the process of creating this book.

About the Author

La Shuana Cole was diagnosed with cancer of the retinas in 1991 at three months old. After undergoing radiation treatment, La Shuana was left with partial vision in her left eye and no vision in her right eye.

In 2012, while a student at the University of Hartford, La Shuana was diagnosed with bone cancer, which forced her to pause her studies to undergo chemotherapy and tumor-removal surgery.

By 2013, La Shuana was cancer-free and had returned to the University of Hartford. She made the Dean's List at the College of Arts and Sciences and received a student leadership award before graduating with a Bachelor of Arts in Politics and Government.

La Shuana later attended New York Law School. In 2021, she graduated with a Juris Doctorate degree and again, with Dean's List and other honors. Later that year, after passing the New York State bar exam with a score of 294, La Shuana was admitted as an attorney to the New York State bar

La Shuana now works as a public interest attorney. In her free time, she enjoys studying geography and the United States'Civil War.

Rochelle s a girl like many others
She has a father, mother,
sisters, and brothers

She likes what girls like and
does what girls do
Like manis and pedis and
shopping too

There is ONE thing that sets Rochelle apart
It's obvious to see, right from the start

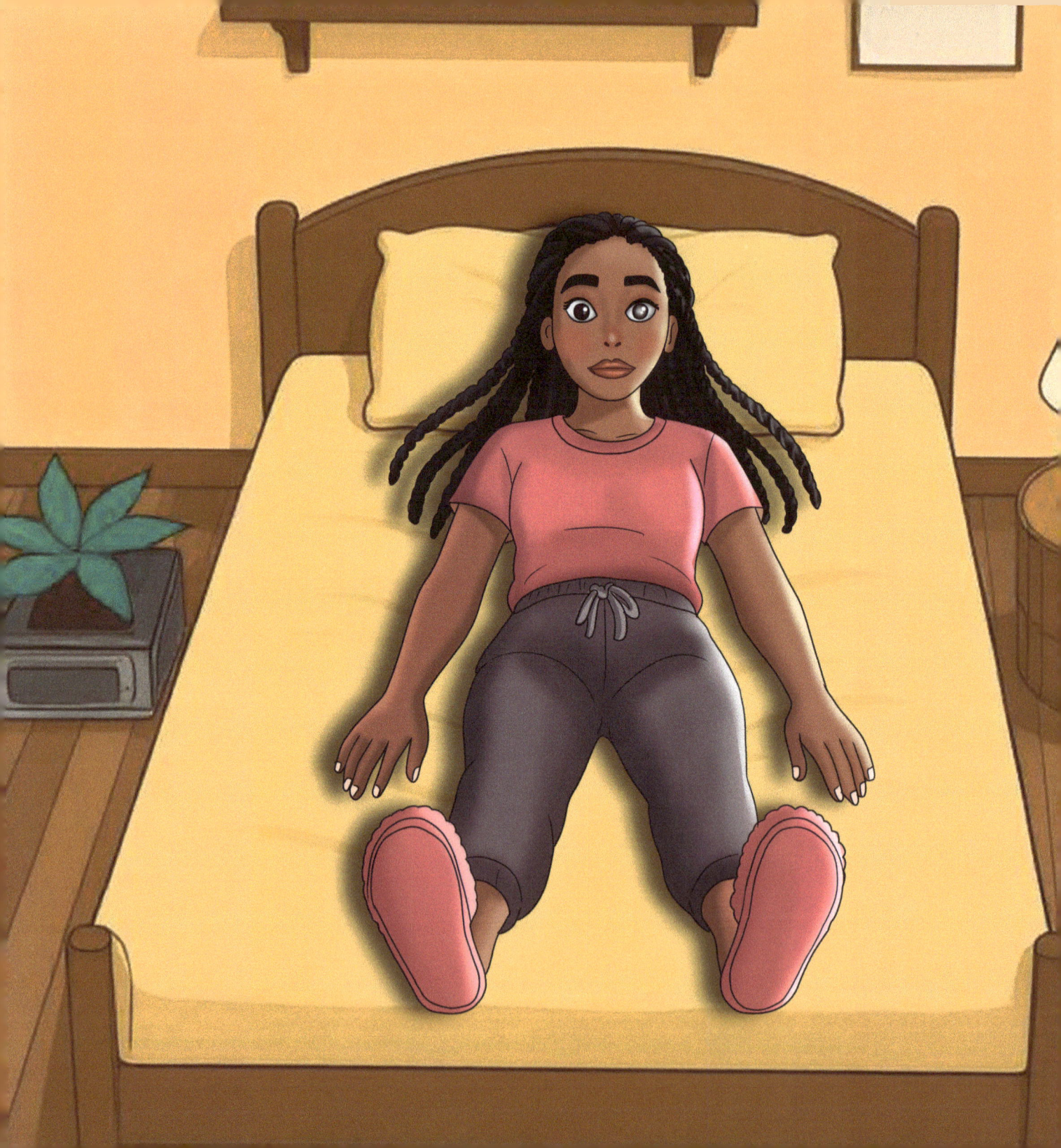

Her eyes look different from those of many
One eye has some vision in the other, not any

While in the vision department,
she may have been slighted
Her senses of hearing and smell
are highlighted

But does low vision stop her?
No way, no how
She never stopped then and she
never stops now
With the vision she has, she
packs up her clothes, her shoes,
her bags, her boxes and bows

She gets up and goes to places
near and far
By bus, by train, by plane, by car

Sometimes with another but
mostly solo
Rochelle won't wait she'll plan
then she'll go

To the Mall in Minnesota
To places in Queens
To the spa in New Jersey
To see New Orleans

From the Mississippi River
To the Caribbean Sea
To the Pacific Coast and the
Hills of Beverly
The Las Vegas Strip with its
casinos and lights
And these are only some places
to which Rochelle has taken
flight

From Rodeo Drive
To the Washington Mall
The Pier in Santa Monica
And that's not even all

From Hollywood Boulevard with
the stars on the ground
To the boroughs of New York
City, up and downtown
Even the Islands of Hawaii with
tasty pineapples, beautiful
sunsets and beaches
Are among the many places that
Rochelle reaches

She plans her routes and executes
With one eye of vision, courage and ambition
Some may wonder, how is this possible?
Then they learn that Rochelle's unstoppable

Low vision won't hold Rochelle
back
Her vision is limited but that s
all she lacks

She wants to experience, see,
learn and do
Just like him, her, them, and you

So even with one eye of vision,
she makes her way
To places and parts from New
York to L.A.

So let this be a lesson to everyone
That having low vision does not mean you're done

You can go, see, and do things
just as well
If you doubt that even a little,
think of Rochelle

www.ingramcontent.com/pod-product-compliance
Lightning Source LLC
Chambersburg PA
CBHW041128120626
46547CB00019B/2903